# better together*

*This book is best read together, grownup and kid.

 akidsco.com

a kids book about

# a kids book about FOSTER ADOPTION

by Jamie Murnane

# a kids book about

Text and design copyright © 2024
by A Kids Book About, Inc.

Copyright is good! It ensures that work like this can exist, and more work in the future can be created.

All rights reserved. No part of this publication may be reproduced, distributed, or transmitted in any form or by any means, including photocopying, recording, other electronic or mechanical methods, without the prior written permission of the publisher, except in the case of brief quotations embodied in critical reviews and certain other noncommercial uses permitted by copyright law. For permission requests, write to the publisher.

A Kids Book About, Kids Are Ready, and the colophon 'a' are trademarks of A Kids Book About, Inc.

Printed in the United States of America.

A Kids Book About books are available online: *akidsco.com*

To share your stories, ask questions, or inquire about bulk purchases (schools, libraries, and nonprofits), please use the following email address: *hello@akidsco.com*

Print ISBN: 979-8-89281-054-8
Ebook ISBN: 979-8-89281-055-5

Designed by Rick DeLucco
Edited by Jennifer Goldstein and Emma Wolf

For my daughter, Dylan.

# Intro

Most kids today understand that families come in various forms. Kids get that all family structures are valid, whether they involve a mom and dad, 2 moms, 2 dads, stepparents, grandparents, or any other combination of relatives. What many kids may not be familiar with is the process of forming families through foster adoption, or adoption from foster care. While adoption books often focus on babies, it's essential to highlight that older kids in foster care, often with complex experiences, also seek permanent, loving families.

It's important for kids in the foster care system (numbering up to 400,000 in the US) to know about possible outcomes for them, and to know that any decision made is made by a judge, supported by a legal and care infrastructure designed to protect them, not by the grownups in their lives. It's also helpful when kids in the system or those who have been adopted from foster care have understanding friends, classmates, and teachers who also know that love is what makes a family.

I'd like to tell you a little bit about
## FOSTER ADOPTION,

and the **foster care system**.

My wife and I knew we wanted to adopt a kid and grow our family.

Because we are both women, we talked a lot about how that could happen.

We first thought about open adoption.

That's when people hoping to adopt are reviewed by an adoption agency.

# SO, WHAT DOES THAT MEAN?

FOR US, IT MEANT COMPLETING A VERY, VERY LONG APPLICATION.

WE SHARED INFORMATION ABOUT WHO WE ARE, WHERE WE LIVE, WHAT WE DO, AND HOW WE EARN MONEY.

WE WENT TO THE DOCTOR FOR A CHECKUP TO SHOW WE WERE HEALTHY ENOUGH TO RAISE A CHILD.

WE TALKED TO THE AGENCY ABOUT OUR RELATIONSHIP WITH ONE ANOTHER, AND OUR FRIENDS AND FAMILY, WHO WOULD HELP US IF WE ADOPTED.

> WE EVEN PRESSED OUR FINGERS ON AN INK PAD, TO LEAVE OUR FINGERPRINTS BEHIND.

Why?

Because everyone's fingerprints are different, like a secret code. An agency can use fingerprints to determine whether we are safe people.

## WE ALSO DID A LOT OF TALKING.

We were interviewed as a couple, on our own, and people who know us told the agency all about us too. It was kind of like trying to get hired for a job!

During this time,
we moved to California...

**so then we did the whole process all over again!**

That's because each state has its own requirements to ensure hopeful adoptive parents are safe people.

Also during this time is when we learned about foster care and the possibility of **foster adoption**.

**Do you know what that means?**

# FOSTER CARE IS...

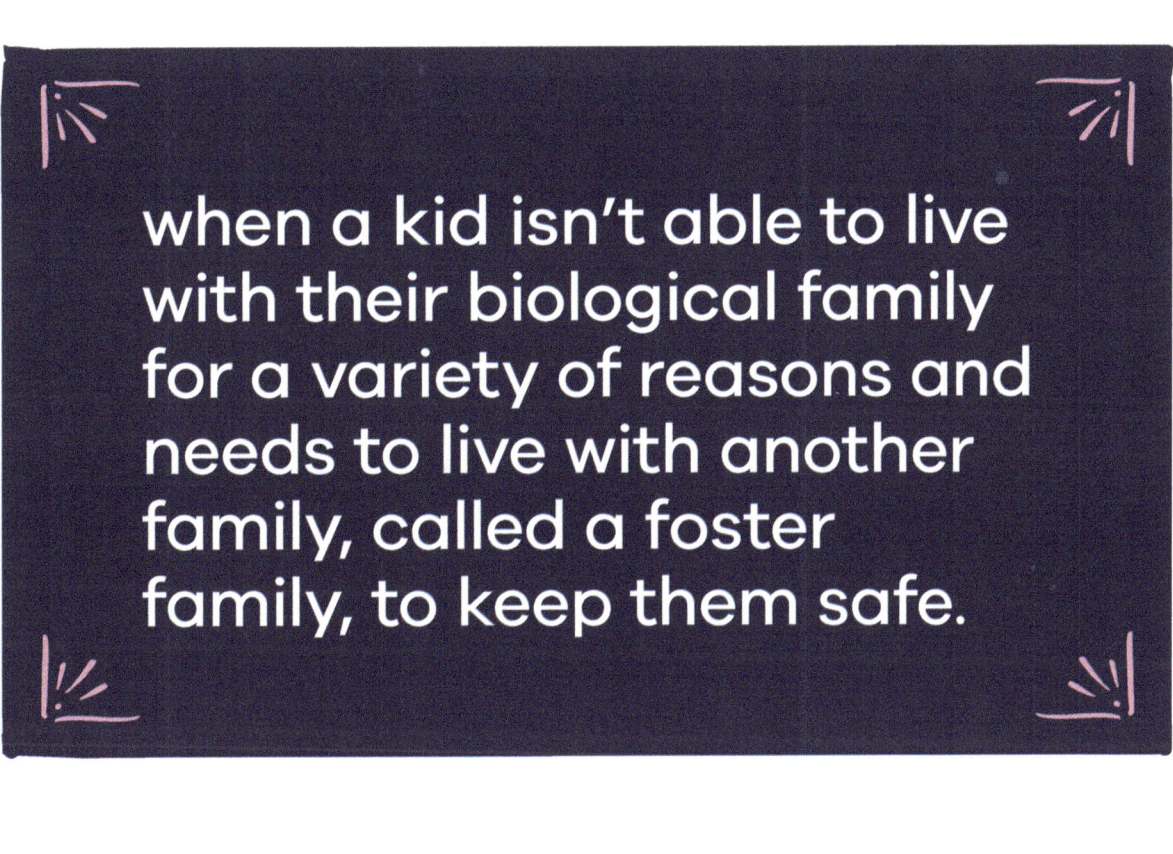

Foster care helps kids whose grownups are having trouble with:

* UNCONTROLLED MENTAL HEALTH ISSUES,

* ADDICTION TO ALCOHOL, DRUGS, OR OTHER SUBSTANCES,

* BEING SAFE WITH THEIR BODIES,

* HITTING OR YELLING INSTEAD OF TALKING,

* ABUSE OF ANY KIND,

* LEAVING THEIR KIDS ALONE WITH NO HELP FOR LONG PERIODS OF TIME,

* PROVIDING A SAFE PLACE TO LIVE EVERY DAY,

* TAKING MONEY THAT DOESN'T BELONG TO THEM,

* HURTING OTHER PEOPLE,

* OR CARING FOR THEIR KIDS BECAUSE THEY ARE INCARCERATED.

Foster care is meant to be temporary with the goal of kids reuniting with their birth families, but when that can't happen, kids need a new, permanent family.

THIS HAPPENS THROUGH FOSTER ADOPTION.

More than

000 kids are in foster care in the United States.

Los Angeles, where we live, has one of the biggest foster care systems in the country.

When my wife and I learned this, we knew we wanted to adopt this way.

WE COULD MAKE OUR
DREAM COME TRUE
AND HELP A KID
(OR KIDS) WHO
NEED IT MOST.

So, how do the foster care
and foster adoption systems work?

GREAT QUESTION!

**In the foster care system**, a kid has a whole team looking out for them.

The team includes social workers, therapists, judges, lawyers, doctors, and other health care professionals.

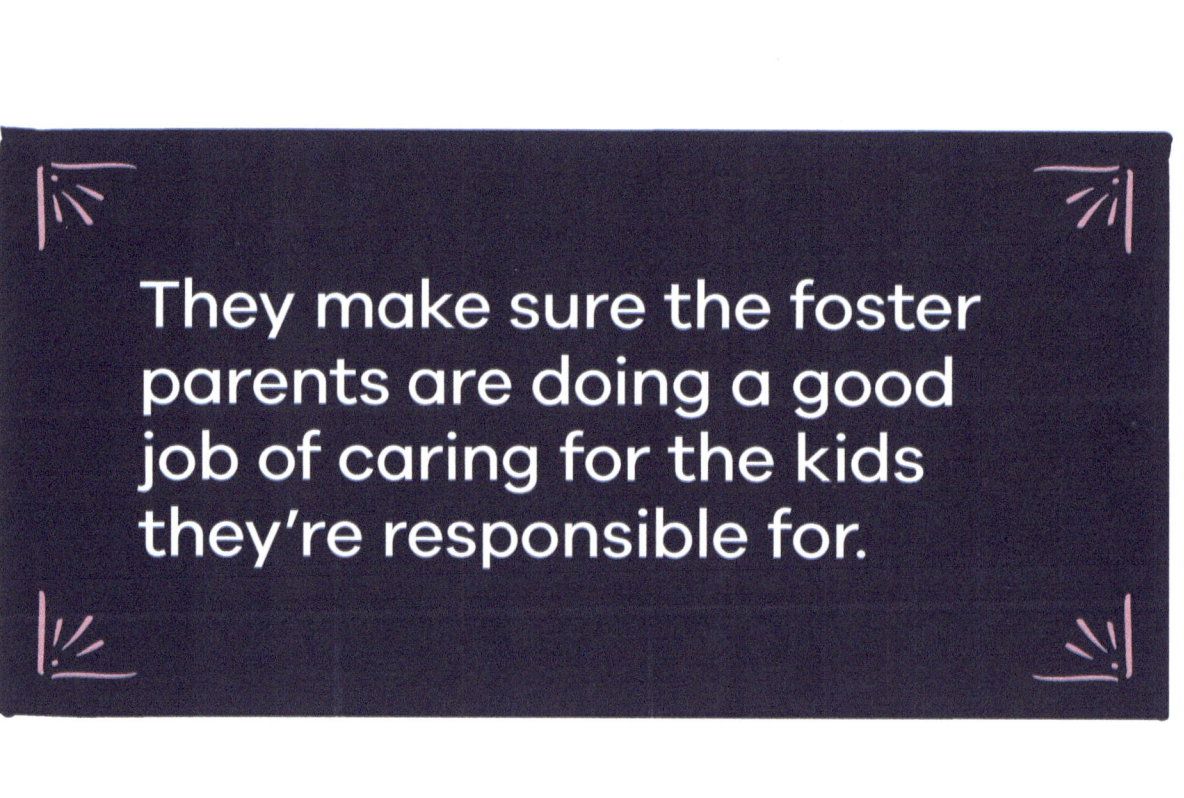

They also make sure a kid's birth family has gotten help with the things that made their kid unsafe in their care.

Often, that means they complete classes to learn better ways to handle themselves, their mental health, or addiction issues, and can show they are able to meet their kids' needs.

2 possible outcomes for
the kid are then considered.

**1.** The first is that they are safely reunited with their birth family.

**2.** The second possibility is that a permanent adoption with a different family needs to take place.

**Not all foster parents adopt.**

Some foster families want to help many kids for a short time, and for several reasons can't grow their family permanently.

We fostered 3 kids, who were each adopted by other people.

We are so happy for them. But it was really hard to say goodbye!

**That's part of the journey for both foster kids and parents.**

Fast-forward to now, and our family permanently includes 1 more person—our daughter!

WE ARE SO HAPPY AS A FAMILY.

She was with another foster family when her care team determined that she could not return safely to her birth family.

Because the foster family she was living with could only help kids for a short time, that meant the team needed to find another foster family who wanted to adopt.

# ENTER

*US!*

But, not so fast!
It isn't that simple.

Our daughter did come to live with us right away, but we weren't able to adopt her for another **4.5 years**!

**Why?** Because it can take a really, really long time for an adoption case to make it through all the steps.

A case is filed, reviewed, corrected, reaches a dead-end, starts over, mistakes are fixed, missing documents are found, and all of this happens through a busy court system.

**This was super hard.**

Our daughter kept asking when she would be adopted, and we couldn't give her an answer.

We knew we wanted to adopt her, but we weren't the ones making the final decision.

So, we waited a long time.

**Waiting is hard, isn't it?**

We read a book with our daughter every night called *Maybe Days*. It helped her understand why everything was taking so long and felt so uncertain.

But then...

# THE DAY ARRIVED!

The day our daughter's adoption was finalized was very exciting.

We cried tears of joy, ate ice cream, and had a kitchen dance party.

We were happy to know
our family was...

# FORE

# VER.

Plus, our kid still has contact with her birth family. This is not always the case, but after adoption is final, the grownups get to decide things without a judge.

And we're glad that while her family has changed, it's grown to make room for even more love.

AND LOVE IS WHAT IT'S ALL ABOUT.

# Outro

Thanks for reading a little bit about my family's journey through foster care, which ultimately led to the adoption of our daughter. While I'd like to say you now know everything about foster adoption, the reality is that each and every scenario is different. The basic setup of team members and the court procedures are relatively similar from state to state, though no 2 foster care or foster adoption cases are alike.

Our daughter's adoption took several years to finalize, but we have friends who had newborns placed with them and adoptions that took less than a year! Some kids, like ours, have ongoing relationships with birth families—others don't.

The world of foster adoption can come with a lot of unknowns and surprises. But there's a very important thing that's not unknown: kids need love, care, stability, and safety. If you've picked up this book, chances are you're already doing a great job at providing those things, so just keep it up.

If you'd like to help or learn more, I encourage you to reach out to your local child welfare agency to find out how you can get started.

## About The Author

Jamie Murnane (she/her) was a foster parent in Los Angeles, California, for 7 years before adopting her daughter. During the years it took for the adoption to become official, she searched to find families like hers reflected in kids' books. Some books included 2 moms, like her family, and some talked about adopting babies. But almost none covered adoption through foster care.

While each foster scenario is unique, Jamie and her daughter felt the world needed a book to understand how families like theirs came to be. She hopes it helps other kids (or their friends and classmates) make sense of everything.

 @j_murn

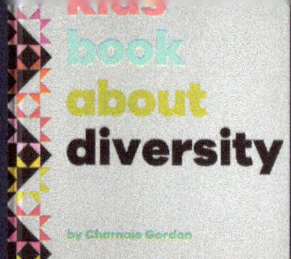

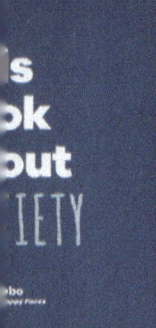
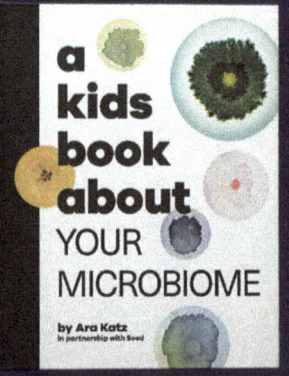

Discover more at akidsco.com

www.ingramcontent.com/pod-product-compliance
Lightning Source LLC
Chambersburg PA
CBHW061359010526
44107CB00012B/986